Dedication

To all the budding scientists and their enthusiastic querries. To the doctors and healers of the future. To every child and their innate curiosity. with love.

Acknowledgements

Westend Writers NC
&
Dr. Kamran Dar

Contents

Overview of the Human Body

Our bodies contain many parts. They work together to make us healthy.

- ➤ We move with our legs
- ➤ Pick things up with our hands
- ➤ See with our eyes
- ➤ Hear with our ears
- ➤ Feel with our skin.

We can see these parts of our body. Others are inside of us, and we cannot see them. We cannot see our liver, brain, and stomach. There are more that we cannot see. We visit the doctor when we don't feel okay, and the doctor checks our body.

Some tiny objects called cells are important to everybody. These cells come together to become tissue. Tissue forms organs, and organs form systems.

For example, we have our excretory systems. They remove waste from our bodies. Let's go on to learn about all the systems that we have in our body.

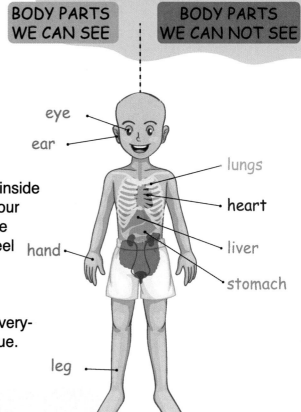

BODY PARTS WE CAN SEE

BODY PARTS WE CAN NOT SEE

eye

ear

lungs

heart

liver

hand

stomach

leg

The Skeletal System

Our body rest on a frame called the skeleton. The skeleton comprises of bones, cartilages, and ligaments. Ligaments join bones together. Bones are hard while cartilage is not so hard. They hold the body upright, keeping our organs safe, helping us move, storing fats, and producing cells for our blood

Classification of Bones

Not all bones are made the same way. Some are long, while some are wide. They also come in many shapes and structures.

Long Bones

- They are long but not wide.

- They contain a long tube that stores fat.

- Long bones are in our legs and arms.

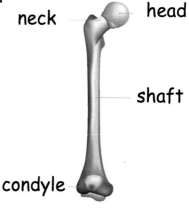

FEMUR (Bone of thigh)

Short Bones

- They are short and look like cubes.

- They have the same lengths and widths.

- They are in our wrists and ankles..

Phalanges (Bones of finger)

Flat Bones

flat bone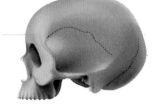

- They are very wide, thin, and flat.

- They cover large areas like our head..

Skull (Bones of head)

Irregular Bones

- They don't have a standard length, shape, or width.

- The spine, hips, and skull have many irregular bones.

body of
vertebra

spinal cord

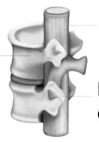

bony process
of vertebra

Vertebra (Bones of back)

Structure of Bone Tissue

There are two bone tissues. One is Compact and the other Spongy. Compact bone tissue is strong and dense, while Spongy is less dense and light. You can find Compact bone tissues in the tubes of long bones. However, Spongy bone tissues are normally found at the two ends of long bones.

Bone tissues have three cells in common. These are:

- Osteoblasts- These are cells that form bones.

- Osteoclasts- These cells break down bones.

- Osteocytes- They are fully-grown bone cells.

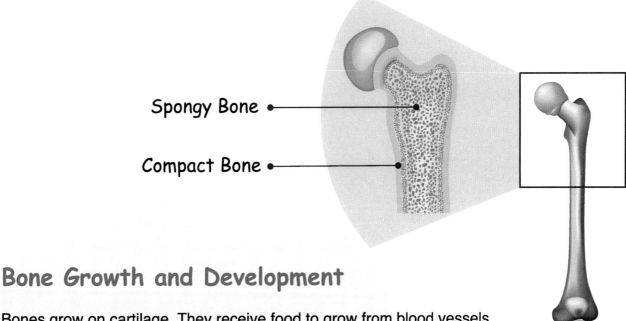

Spongy Bone

Compact Bone

Bone Growth and Development

Bones grow on cartilage. They receive food to grow from blood vessels through nutrient holes. Bones grow a lot in children. In adults, bones don't grow as much. New bones grow when old ones need repairing.

Joints

Joints are part of the skeletal system. They are points where two or more bones meet. Joints also help in movement.

There are three types of joints.

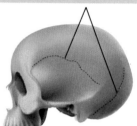

Immovable Joints of skull

Immovable Joints:

- They allow no movement at all.

- Bones are rigidly held together by fibers.

- The suture joints in our skulls are immovable joints..

Slightly moveable:

- They allow some movement.

- Bones are held by cartilage.

- Examples of these are joints in the column of the spine.

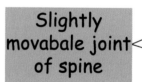

Slightly movabale joint of spine

Freely moveable:

- Bones held together by a type of fluid.

- For instance, the Ball and Socket joint in our hip moves in all directions, while the hinge joint in our knees can only go back and forth.

Ball & Socket Joint of hip

Muscles

Muscles help us to move, breathe, and digest our foods. We have three types of muscles. They are:

1. Skeletal

2. Cardiac

3. Smooth muscles.

Skeletal Muscles:

> Our bodies have many skeletal muscles.

> Each of us has over 600 skeletal muscles.

> They help bones to move over the body by contracting and relaxing.

> We can control them with our thought, so they are also known as Voluntary

Skeletal Muscle

Smooth Muscles:

> Our organs also have smooth muscles. For example, our stomach digests food using smooth muscles.

> We cannot control these muscles with our thought. Hence, they are Involuntary muscles.

Smooth Muscle

Cardiac Muscles:

> Cardiac muscles surround the heart.

> They help our heart to pump blood.

> We cannot control them, either.

Cardiac Muscle

Now that we know the three types of muscles, let's talk about how these muscles work in different parts of our bodies.

Head & Neck:

We can pull faces because we have muscles. They also help us to chew, nod, and shake our heads. The muscles used for chewing are very strong.

Trunk:

We have three groups of muscles in our trunk. They cover our spine, chest & tummy, and hips. The muscles in our spine help us to stand erect. We breathe with the help of muscles in our chest and tummy. Muscles in our hips help our hip bones to move.

Upper Extremity:

These are muscles in our shoulders, forearms, lower arms, wrists, and hands. They join our shoulder blades to our chests and move our arms, hands, and fingers. Many of these muscles are in our forearms.

Lower Extremity:

All the muscles in the thighs, legs, ankles, feet and gluteus (buttocks) belong to this class. They help us move our thighs and legs. They also help us to bend and straighten our knees and join our buttocks to our thighs

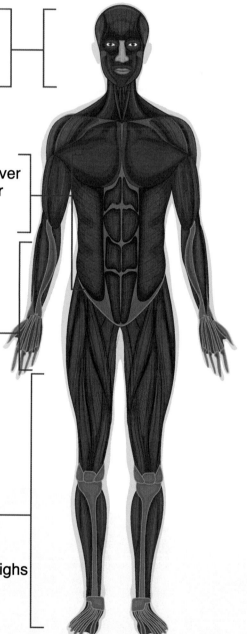

Nervous System

The nervous system controls how we respond to everything in our environment. It contains the central nervous system and peripheral nervous system. Our brain and spinal cord make up the central nervous system. They control the rest of the system. The peripheral obeys the command of our brain and spinal cord. The small cells in the nervous system are called Neurons and Glia.

Neurons are very sensitive. They receive signs from our environment and pass them through our nerves. The signals can be electrical or chemical. Glia cells assist the neurons. A neuron has a big head, branches called dendrites, and a long tail (axon).

dendrites

nucleus myelin sheath axon

axon terminal

The Synapse:

We have many neurons, and they act together. The axon terminal has small branches. These branches send signals to the long branches of dendrites through small gaps. The small gaps are called synapses. Neurons cannot pass messages to one another without synapses.

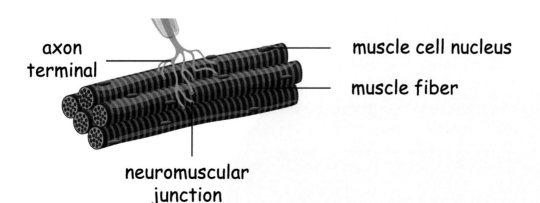

axon terminal

muscle cell nucleus

muscle fiber

neuromuscular junction

Sense Organs

Our sense organs connect us with our environment. They work with the nervous systems. The sense organs pick up messages from the environment and send them to the nervous system. The sense organs are discussed below.

Eyes:

We see with our eyes. The white part of our eyes is the sclera. The dark center is the iris and it controls the amount of light that enters our eyes. The pupil is at the center of the iris and it serves as the opening for light to enter. The retina is found behind these visible parts. All these parts collect light signals and send them to the brain. The brain then makes images from them.

Nose:

We smell with our noses. We have hairs inside our nostrils. They pick up signs from the environment and send them to the brain for command..

Ears:

We hear with our ears. Our ears stretch inside until they connect with the brain. The curved outer parts of our ears collect signals from the outside and guide them inside and to the brain. The brain then processes them into sounds for us..

Tongue:

Our tongue is a big mass of muscles. We use it for tasting. Our tongue has tiny bumps called taste buds. Our taste buds pick up signals whenever we put something on our tongue. The signals are then sent to the brain for further commands.

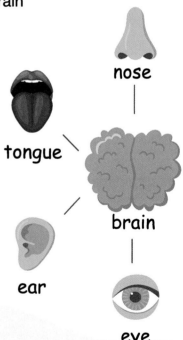

nose

tongue

brain

ear

eye

Cardiovascular System

Our blood is that reddish substance that flows out of our body whenever our skin opens up because we've hurt ourselves. It carries oxygen and food all over our body. It also carries the body soldiers that protect us. Although blood looks like red water it is not empty. About 55% of blood is plasma. Plasma contains water, dissolved nutrients, hormones and many other important things.

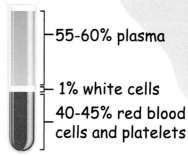

—55-60% plasma

— 1% white cells
— 40-45% red blood cells and platelets

Constituents of Blood

Parts of the Heart:

The Heart pumps blood for us. It has four chambers that move blood between the lungs and the rest of the body. They are called: left and right ventricles and atria (singular atrium). It also has some valves that open and close to control the flow of blood.

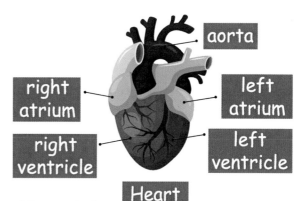

aorta

right atrium

left atrium

right ventricle

left ventricle

Heart

Blood Circulation:

Blood moves from the heart to and from the lungs and the rest of the body. Our arteries carry blood with oxygen. Our veins carry blood without oxygen. They exchange in the capillaries.

Types of Cells in Blood:

- Red Blood Cells

- White Blood Cells

- Platelets

Red Blood Cell

Platelet

White Blood Cell

Lymphatic System

Our lymphatic system works with our circulatory and immune systems. It works in two phases.

The first is to collect any excess fluid left in our bodies.

The second is to get rid of germs and unwanted materials.

Many vessels, nodes, and organs are in our lymphatic system. The lymph is the fluid of the system. The lymph goes through our lymph nodes and organs for cleansing before moving back into the bloodstream.

Tonsils:

Tonsils are the two fleshy mounds hanging down our throat. They catch germs entering from our mouth and nose.

Spleen:

It is the biggest organ in the lymphatic system. It makes white blood cells and cleanses the blood as it passes through it.

Lymph Nodes:

They produce some white blood cells that fight the body's germs. They also clean up damaged body cells and cancerous cells.

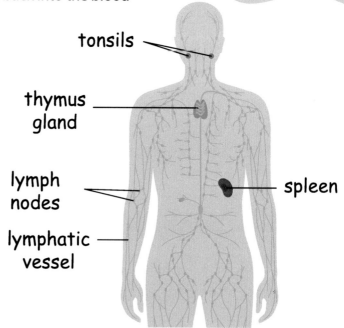

tonsils

thymus gland

lymph nodes

lymphatic vessel

spleen

Connections of the Lymphatic System

Digestive System

We need nutrients to survive. That is why we eat. However, food contains these nutrients in forms that the body cannot absorb. Hence, the body must break these complex nutrients into simple forms that we can use.

Teeth:

The first stage of digestion happens in our mouth. Teeth are strong bones that we use when chewing food. Chewing helps to reduce the size of the food. It allows the chemicals in our saliva to cover all of the food in our mouth.

Salivary Glands:

Salivary glands produce saliva. Saliva has essential chemicals called Amylase that break down the food in our mouths. Once our teeth break down the food, saliva mixes with it.

Esophagus:

The esophagus is a long tube that runs from the mouth to the stomach. Our tongue rolls the chewed food down the esophagus, which in turn moves it further down by contracting and relaxing its muscles. The end of the tube, towards the stomach, has a valve which shuts once the food enters so that it cannot go back to the mouth

Stomach:

This sac-like organ contains many chemicals and acids to digest food into simpler forms and to destroy germs found in food. It then sends the food broken down into bits to the intestine. After about two to six hours, all digested food will be moved to the intestines..

Intestines:

Our body has two intestines:
  The small intestine

  The large intestine.

Small Intestine:

The small intestine has three parts where food from the stomach gets further digested. Final food breakdown and nutrient absorption into the body take place in the small intestine. The body sucks nutrients using devices that look like the fingers. They are called villi.

Large Intestine:

The large intestine collects any material that the small intestine cannot digest and further removes water out of them. The remaining wastes are then stored until we pass them out as feces through the anus.

It is the largest organ inside the body. It helps with digestion, but it also removes waste. The liver produces a bitter greenish fluid called bile which breaks down fat. The gallbladder is the bile storehouse.

Pancreas:

It produces a juice with many chemicals that break down food inside the small intestine.

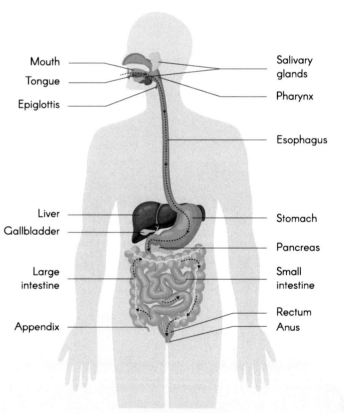

Mouth
Tongue
Epiglottis
Salivary glands
Pharynx
Esophagus
Liver
Gallbladder
Stomach
Pancreas
Large intestine
Small intestine
Rectum
Anus
Appendix

Digestive Tract

Urinary System

Our body must always remain stable. The urinary system helps it do that. We also use this system to remove waste.

Kidneys:

We have two kidneys shaped like beans with many tubes called nephrons, the functional part of the kidney. They filter the blood and regulate all solutes in the body, with the exception of proteins.

Bladder:

It stores the filtrate from the kidneys. Once the bladder gets full, we pass it out by urinating.

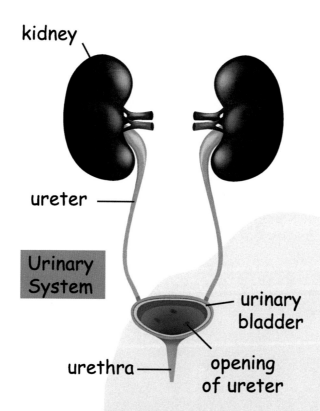

kidney

ureter

Urinary System

urinary bladder

urethra

opening of ureter

Immune System

How it works:

We come into contact with germs every second of the day. Our immune system is made up of cells that act like soldiers for our body fighting these germs so that we do not fall ill every time. Once the cells sense trouble, they rush to the site, they get to know the germs, they fight them, and then stop once the germs are killed so that they do not harm the body cells. They also store the encounter in their memory so that they know how to defend the body from the same germs in the future.

The task of the immune system:

The primary task of the immune system is to keep out germs (for example, bacteria, viruses, parasites, fungi) that can make us sick. It does this by identifying the germs, grouping them, killing them, and remembering the process for the future. It also fights against diseases that can change our body cells, such as cancer.

How the immune system is activated:

Our body cells have proteins on them, whereas the immune cells have special agents on their surfaces called receptors. These receptors recognize proteins and determine who they are. That is why they do not attack normal body cells.

In the same way, germs have proteins on their bodies called antigens. Once these antigens touch the receptors, the immune system recognizes that it is not from normal body cells and gets activated.

However, the immune cells sometimes fail to recognize our body cells' proteins and attack them. Such cases are called autoimmune disease.

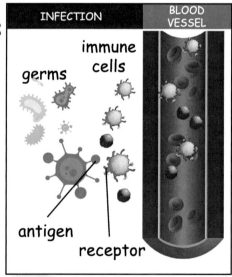

Word Definitions

- **Bones**- The hardest part of the skeletal system

- **Cartilage**- Soft and less rigid part of the skeletal system

- **Cell**- the smallest unit of life

- **Complex**- something difficult to understand

- **Digest**- to break into small pieces

- **Ligament**- joins bones together

- **Organ**- a group of tissues with the same function

- **Peripheral**- an attachment

- **Receptors**- anything that can receive

- **Rigid**- something hard that does not move

- **System**- a group of organs with the same function

- **Tissue**- a group of cells with the same function

References

1. Lumen Biology for Majors II, Module 23: The Musculoskeletal System. Accessed 25 October, 2021. https://courses.lumenlearning.com/wm-biology2/chapter/types-of-bone/

2. SEER Training Modules, Anatomy and Physiology. U. S. National Institutes of Health, National Cancer Institute. Accessed 26 October, 2021. https://training.seer.cancer.gov/anatomy/skeletal/growth.html

3. Visible Body. Bones Come Together: Types of Joints in the Human Body.   Accessed 26 October, 2021. https://www.visiblebody.com/learn/skeleton/joints-and-ligaments

4. Visible Body. 5 Facts about Human Muscles: An Overview of the Muscular System and How Muscles Move. Accessed 26 October, 2021. https://www.visiblebody.com/learn/muscular/muscular-overview

5. SEER Training Modules, Anatomy and Physiology. U. S. National Institutes of Health, National Cancer Institute. Accessed 26 October, 2021. https://training.seer.cancer.gov/anatomy/muscular/groups/head_neck.html

6. SEER Training Modules, Anatomy and Physiology. U. S. National Institutes of Health, National Cancer Institute. Accessed 26 October, 2021. https://training.seer.cancer.gov/anatomy/muscular/groups/trunk.html

7. SEER Training Modules, Anatomy and Physiology. U. S. National Institutes of Health, National Cancer Institute. Accessed 26 October, 2021. https://training.seer.cancer.gov/anatomy/muscular/groups/lower.html

8. Cherry K. (2020). Synapses in the Nervous System: Where Nerve Impulses Are Passed from Neuron to Neuron. Accessed 26 October, 2021. https://www.verywellhealth.com/synapse-anatomy-2795867

9. Cushwa W (n.d). Human Biology. Accessed 26 October, 2021 http://cnx.org/content/col11903/1.3/

10. Visible Body. Brain and Nerves: Five Keys to Unlock the Nervous System. Accessed 26 October, 2021. https://www.visiblebody.com/learn/nervous/system-overview

11. Visible Body. Sight, Sound, Smell, Taste, and Touch: How the Human Body Receives Sensory Information. Accessed 26 October, 2021. https://www.visiblebody.com/learn/nervous/five-senses

12. Visible Body. At the Heart of It All: Anatomy and Function of the Heart. Accessed 26 October, 2021. https://www.visiblebody.com/learn/circulatory/circulatory-the-heart

13. Cleveland Clinic (2020). Lymphatic System. Accessed 26 October, 2021.   https://my.clevelandclinic.org/health/articles/21199-lymphatic-system

14. InfomedHealth.org [Internet]. Cologne, Germany: Institute for Quality and Efficiency in Health Care (IQWiG); 2006-. How does the immune system work?   [Updated 2020 Apr 23]. Accessed 27 October, 2021 https://www.ncbi.nlm.nih.gov/books/NBK279364/

Author's Bio

The author is an educator and a passionate lover of children. He received his Bachelor of Arts in Biology from Edgewood College in Madison. Wisconsin and a second B.A. in Healthcare Management from Southern Illinois University Carbondale where he also completed his M.A in Engineering. He has a wealth of valuable experience dealing with children of varying age ranges. The author does not only love children, but he understands that when they have the best form of education, it has a far-reaching effect on the wider society. As a result, he is on a mission to make sure that children learn as much as they can.

Other Books by Z.B. Tucker

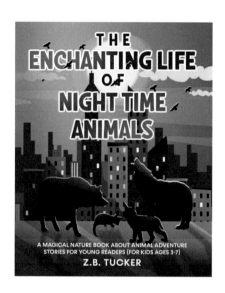

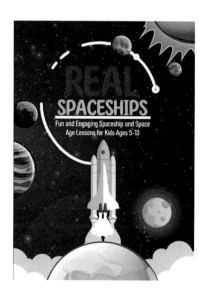

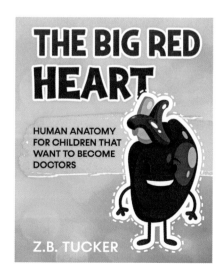

Made in the USA
Las Vegas, NV
25 February 2024